Our Classroom Rules

Nora Sotherden

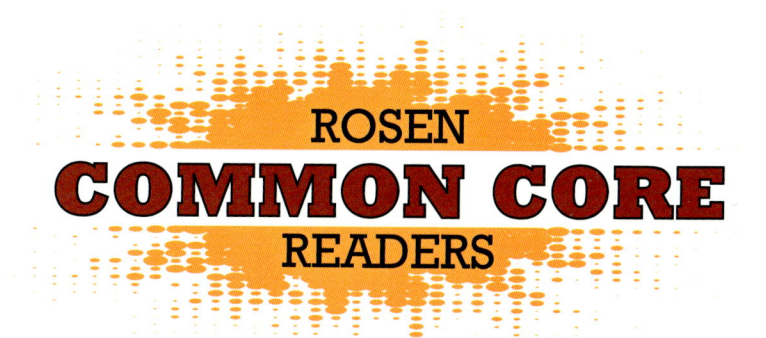

ROSEN
COMMON CORE
READERS

Rosen Classroom™

New York

Published in 2013 by The Rosen Publishing Group, Inc.
29 East 21st Street, New York, NY 10010

Copyright © 2013 by The Rosen Publishing Group, Inc.

All rights reserved. No part of this book may be reproduced in any form without permission in writing from the publisher, except by a reviewer.

Book Design: Michael Harmon

Photo Credits: Cover, p. 5 Zurijeta/Shutterstock.com; p. 7 Nicholas Prior/Taxi/Getty Images; p. 9 Tomasz Trojanowski; p. 11 michaeljung/Shutterstock.com; p. 13 Monkey Business Images/Shutterstock.com; p. 15 Lisa Stirling/Digitial Vision/Getty Images.

ISBN: 978-1-4488-8692-0
6-pack ISBN: 978-1-4488-8693-7

Manufactured in the United States of America

CPSIA Compliance Information: Batch #WS12RC: For further information contact Rosen Publishing, New York, New York at 1-800-237-9932.

Word Count: 38

Contents

Our Classroom Rules   4

Words to Know   16

Index   16

We have rules
in our classroom.

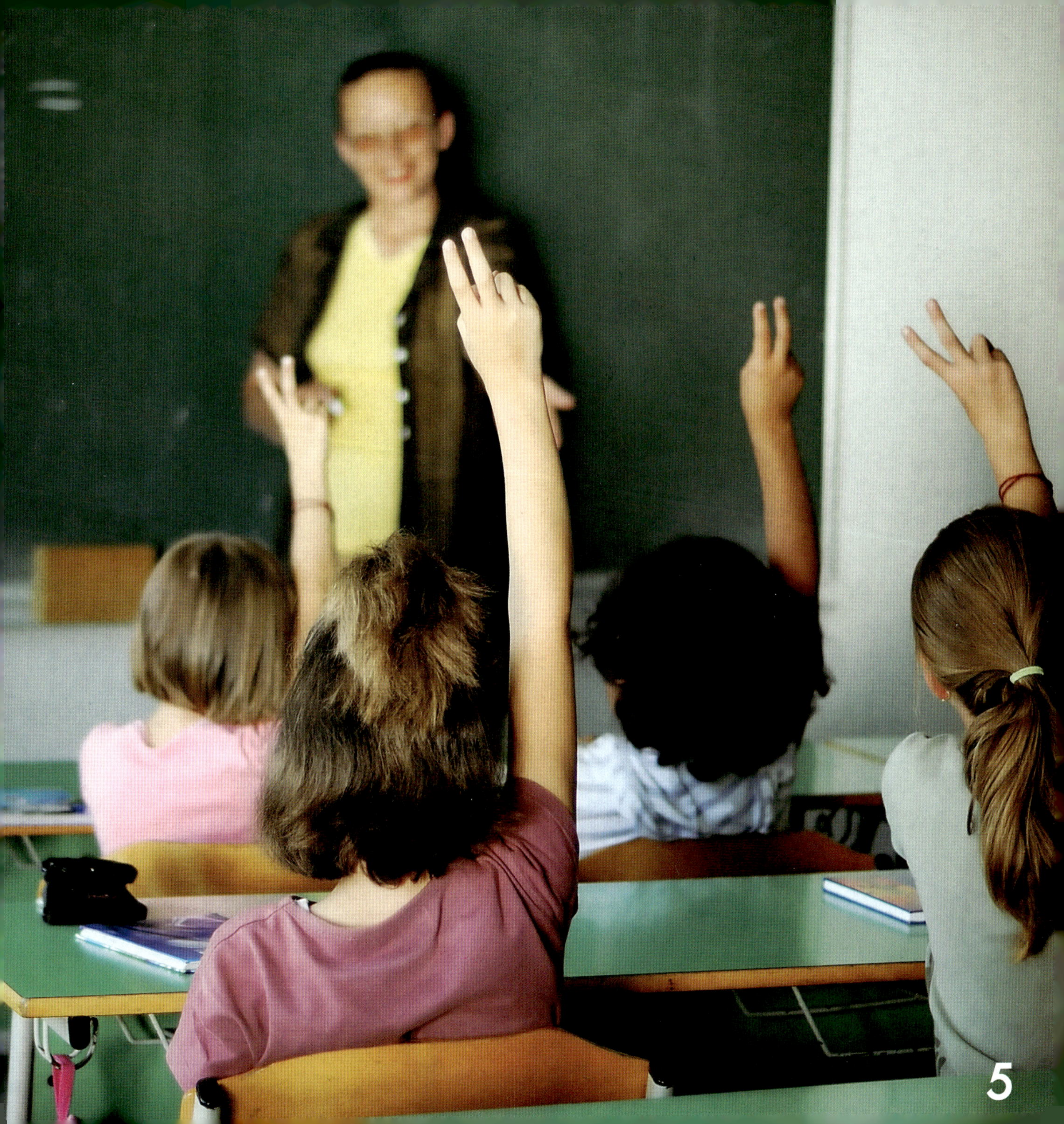

Mary comes to class on time.

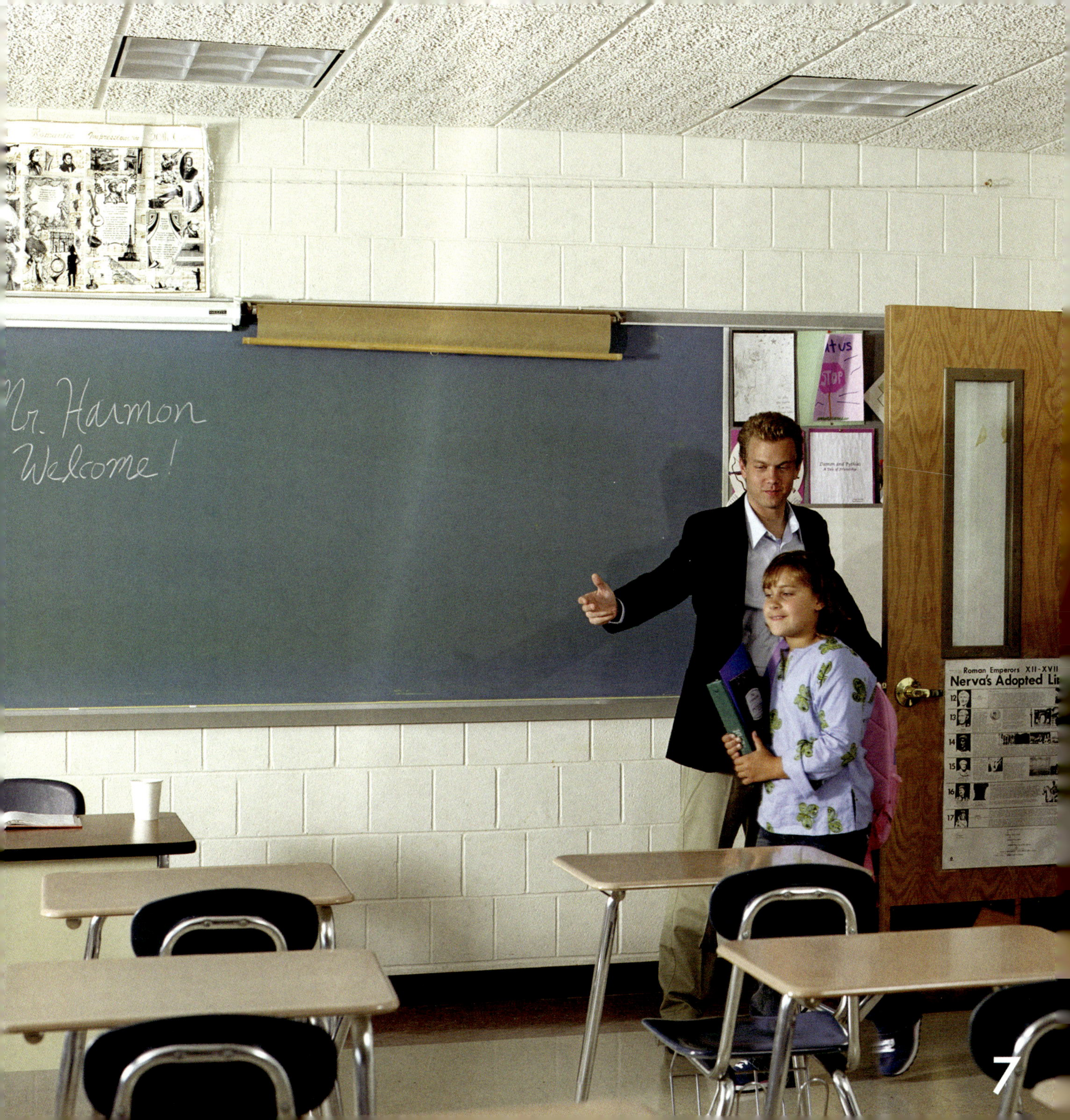
Welcome!
Roman Emperors

Ava waits quietly in the line.

9

John raises his hand during class.

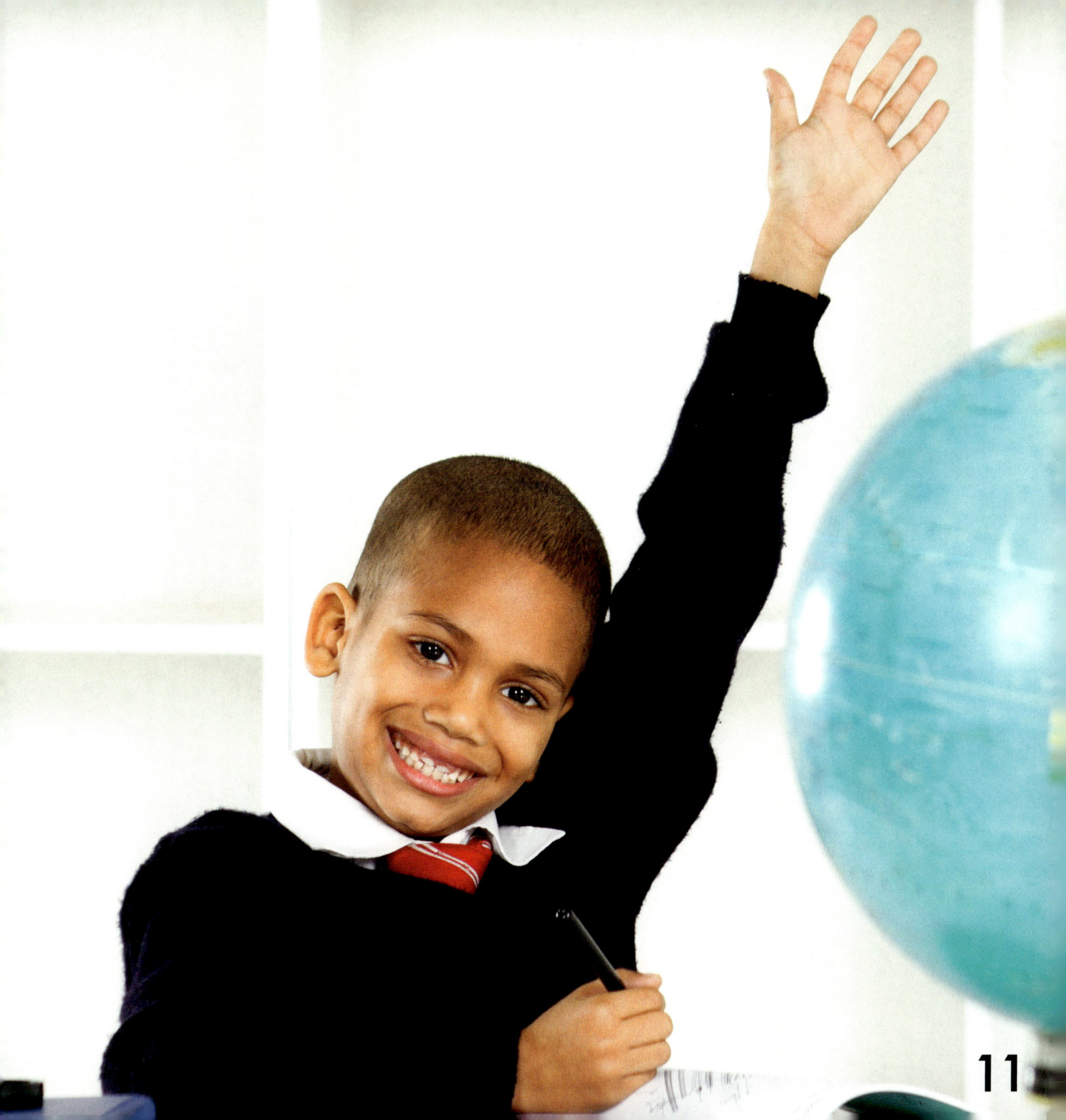

Abby does not yell during class.

Janey cleans up
at the end of class.

Words to Know

classroom

line

Index

class, 6, 10, 12, 14
classroom, 4
hand, 10

line, 8
rules, 4